T0014243

MINDFULNESS AND

TECHNOLOGY

PRISCILLA AN

childsworld.com

The Child's World®
childsworld.com

Published by The Child's World®
800-599-READ · www.childsworld.com

Photography Credits
Photographs ©: Westock Productions/Shutterstock
Images, cover, 1, 7, 8, 11, 12–13; Shutterstock Images, 3, 15,
16–17, 19, 20; Rich Legg/iStockphoto, 4–5; Antonio Diaz/
Shutterstock Images, 22

ISBN Information
9781503869646 (Reinforced Library Binding)
9781503880863 (Portable Document Format)
9781503882171 (Online Multi-user eBook)
9781503883482 (Electronic Publication)
9781645498612 (Paperback)

LCCN 2022951206

Printed in the United States of America

Priscilla An is a children's book editor and author. She lives in Minnesota with her rabbit and likes to practice mindfulness through yoga.

TABLE OF CONTENTS

CHAPTER 1

WHAT IS MINDFULNESS?

Technology has many good uses. It can connect people to others who are far away. It can help people learn new things. People can have fun using technology. But technology can also **distract** people from the present moment. Practicing mindfulness can help. Mindfulness is when people are aware of their thoughts, feelings, and surroundings. Being mindful can help people pause when they are using too much technology. They can notice the signs from their bodies that they need a break from technology.

People of all ages
can use technology.

FIGHTING A DRAGON

Every summer break, Ryan goes to his cousin Sajan's house for a month. They always have a lot of fun together. This time, Sajan has a new video game. Ryan is excited to play.

The boys wake up early on Saturday to play the game. They want extra playing time, because they are meeting friends at the park later. As soon as they start playing, Ryan and Sajan are **hooked**. The game is so fun!

Playing video games can be a lot of fun.

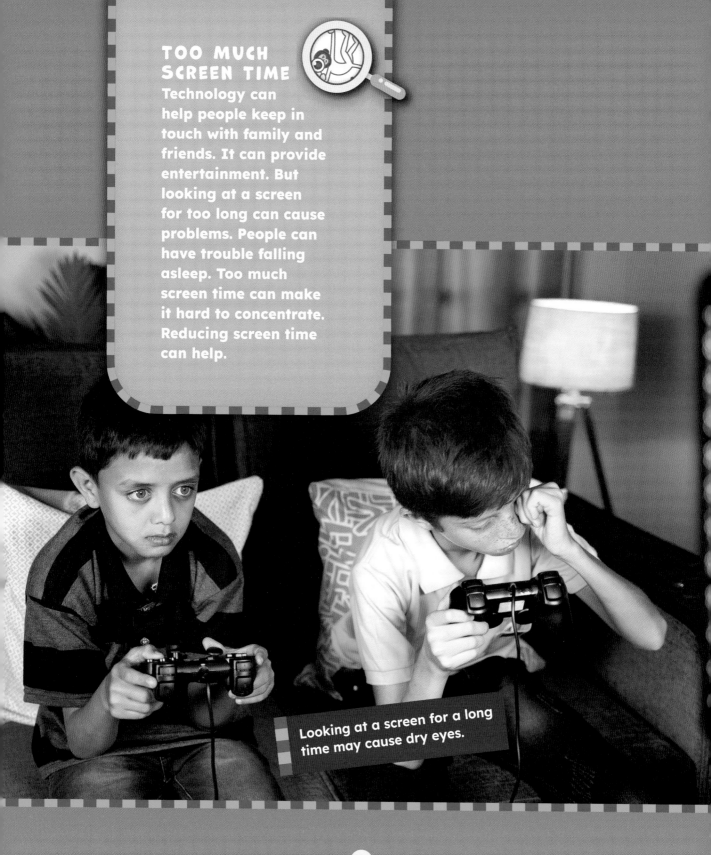

TOO MUCH SCREEN TIME

Technology can help people keep in touch with family and friends. It can provide entertainment. But looking at a screen for too long can cause problems. People can have trouble falling asleep. Too much screen time can make it hard to concentrate. Reducing screen time can help.

Looking at a screen for a long time may cause dry eyes.

Three hours pass. Ryan and Sajan are still playing. They are fighting monsters together. The next monster they will fight is a dragon.

Ryan rubs his eyes. They hurt from staring at the TV screen for so long. But the game is too exciting to stop! "Can we play for one more hour?" he asks Sajan.

"Yeah, we can just finish fighting the dragon," Sajan says.

But fighting the dragon takes longer than they thought it would. Two more hours pass, but they still have not defeated the dragon. Both of their heads are hurting.

Sajan's older brother comes into the room. "You guys are still playing? Your friend Jaya is calling me."

Ryan looks up at the clock and gasps. Time had gone by so quickly! Sajan gets the phone and puts it on speaker mode.

"Where are you guys?" Jaya says. She sounds upset. "You were supposed to be here an hour ago!" The boys apologize. They say they can head to the park now. But their friends are ready to go home. Ryan and Sajan promise to be on time tomorrow.

Sajan looks at Ryan. "Well, we already missed them. Should we keep playing?"

Ryan shakes his head. "My eyes feel like they're burning. Do you want to ride our bikes instead?"

People may lose track of time when they play video games.

"That sounds great!" Sajan leaps from his seat.

As the boys ride their bikes, they set a plan. They want to play the game tomorrow, too. But they will use a timer to keep track of time. Playing the game for too long made their bodies tired. And they did not want to disappoint their friends again.

Going outside is often a nice break from technology.

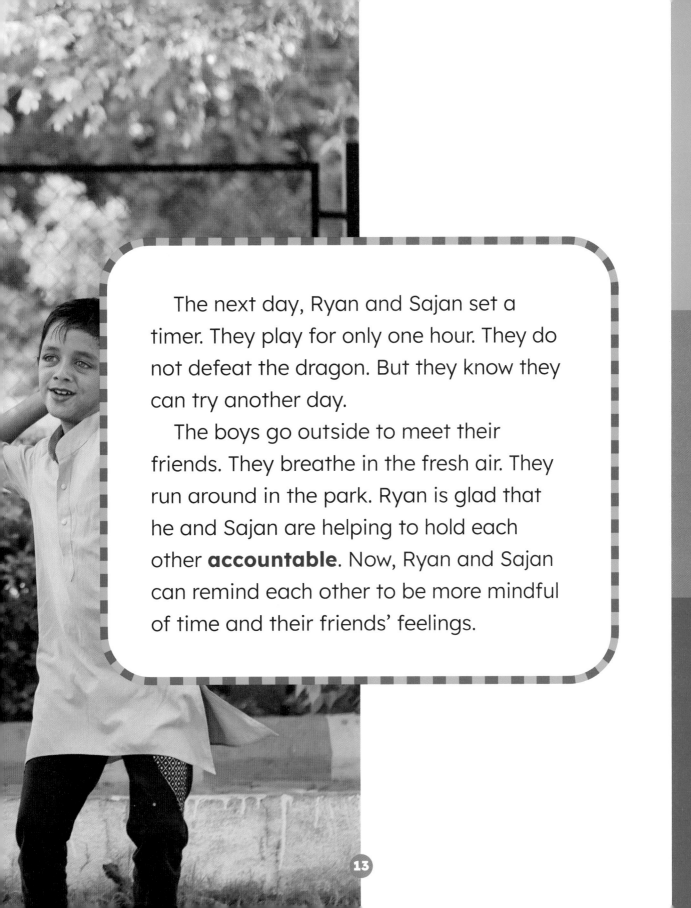

The next day, Ryan and Sajan set a timer. They play for only one hour. They do not defeat the dragon. But they know they can try another day.

The boys go outside to meet their friends. They breathe in the fresh air. They run around in the park. Ryan is glad that he and Sajan are helping to hold each other **accountable**. Now, Ryan and Sajan can remind each other to be more mindful of time and their friends' feelings.

CHAPTER 3

MINDFUL BREAKS

Ava's school handed out laptops this week. Her teachers are now giving homework through the school's website. Ava is excited to use her laptop at home. She likes how the keyboard sounds. It makes her feel like a grown-up!

Ava is doing her math homework on her laptop. This is her third time trying to solve the same problem. The numbers are starting to look blurry on the screen.

Laptops can help people study or work.

Taking breaks can help prevent headaches.

Ava's head and neck hurt. She closes her eyes. Ava feels **stressed**. It is hard to concentrate on her homework. Ava also has other homework to do. She is worried that she will not finish in time.

Ava's dad comes over. "Are you feeling OK, Ava?"

Ava groans. "My eyes hurt. Solving this problem is so hard."

"If your eyes hurt, it's time for you to take a break!" Ava's dad says. "You can drink water and do some stretches. Look at other things instead of the screen."

"But I have so many things to do!" Ava says. She feels **overwhelmed**.

"That means you definitely need a break," her dad says, smiling. "Sometimes, when you feel overwhelmed, a break can help you rest and **focus** better."

Ava nods. She gets up from her seat and takes off her sweater. She rolls her shoulders. She touches her toes. As Ava stretches, she feels her body relax. She jumps up and down and wiggles her body. It feels good to move! Afterward, Ava pours herself a glass of water. She gulps the whole thing down. She feels so refreshed!

After 20 minutes, Ava goes back to her math homework. Her body feels better, but her eyes still hurt. She asks her dad for advice.

"How about writing the problem down in your notebook?" he says. "That way, your eyes will have a break from the screen."

OTHER MINDFUL BREAKS

Doing homework on a screen or going to school online can be hard. There are many ways to take mindful breaks. Besides stretching and drinking water, going outside and getting fresh air can help. Other mindful breaks include dancing, practicing yoga, or eating a snack.

Drinking water helps give people more energy.

Writing on paper can help people remember things better.

Ava writes down her math problem. She finishes the problem easily! Being able to write things down helped a lot. So did resting her eyes. Ava is glad she took a break. She had not even realized she was thirsty. She was so focused on doing her schoolwork that she forgot to take care of her body.

Taking a break gave Ava more energy. Her eyes and neck do not hurt anymore. Ava decides that she will take more mindful breaks in the future. It will make her feel less stressed and overwhelmed.

WONDER MORE

Wondering about New Information

How much did you know about the importance of taking a break from technology before reading this book? What new information did you learn? Write down two new facts that this book taught you. Was the new information surprising? Why or why not?

Wondering How It Matters

What is one way being mindful while using technology relates to your life? How do you think it relates to other kids' lives?

Wondering Why

Taking mindful breaks can help you rest your mind and body. Why do you think it is important to rest your mind and body? How might knowing this affect your life?

Ways to Keep Wondering

Learning about mindfulness and technology can be a complex topic. After reading this book, what questions do you have about it? What can you do to learn more about mindfulness?

YOGA: CHILD'S POSE

Practicing yoga is one way to take a mindful break from technology.

1. Kneel on a blanket or yoga mat.

2. Spread your knees wide, making sure your big toes are touching each other. You can also keep your knees together.

3. Stretch out your arms in front of you with your palms touching the floor. Lean your body all the way forward, pressing your head into the mat.

4. Slowly breathe in through your nose. Breathe out through your mouth. As you breathe, relax your shoulders and close your eyes. You can move your head from side to side to give your forehead a little massage.

5. Continue in this pose until your mind and body feel relaxed.

GLOSSARY

accountable (uh-KOWN-tuh-bull) Being accountable means a person is taking responsibility for his actions. Ryan and Sajan keep each other accountable so they don't play video games for too long.

distract (dih-STRAKT) To distract is to turn someone's attention away from something. Technology can distract people and make them lose track of time.

focus (FOH-kuss) To focus is to pay special attention to something. Ava found it hard to focus on her homework.

hooked (HOOKD) When someone is hooked on an activity, he is focusing his whole attention and interest on it. When Ryan and Sajan started playing their video game, they were hooked.

overwhelmed (oh-vur-WELLMD) When thoughts or feelings become too much to handle, a person can feel overwhelmed. Ava felt overwhelmed when she thought about how many things she had to do.

stressed (STREST) A person who is stressed feels pressured or worried. Ava felt stressed when she could not solve her math problem.

FIND OUT MORE

In the Library

An, Priscilla. *Mindfulness and Nature.*
Parker, CO: The Child's World, 2024.

Lawler, Jean C. *Experience Media: How
Your Media Choices Make You Feel.*
Egremont, MA: Red Chair Press, 2018.

Verde, Susan. *I Am Yoga.* New York, NY: Abrams, 2015.

On the Web

Visit our website for links about mindfulness
and technology:

childsworld.com/links

*Note to Parents, Caregivers, Teachers, and Librarians: We routinely verify our
Web links to make sure they are safe and active sites. So encourage your readers
to check them out!*

INDEX